KENA U

CW00349132

With the Co

ŚAṄKARA

Translated by

Swami Gambhirananda

Advaita Ashrama
(Publication Department)
5 Dehi Entally Road
Kolkata 700 014

Published by
Swami Mumukshananda
President, Advaita Ashrama
Mayavati, Champawat, Himalayas
from its Publication Department, Kolkata
Email: mail@advaitaonline.com
Website: www.advaitaonline.com

© *All Rights Reserved*
Sixth Impression, May 2003
3M3C

ISBN 81-7507-068-3

Printed in India at
Gipidi Box Co.
Kolkata 700 014

PREFACE TO THE THIRD EDITION

This new edition of the *Kena Upaniṣad* has been thoroughly revised by the author himself. In the matter of printing, to facilitate things for the reader, more space is given between the translation of the text and the translation of the *bhāṣya*. In the references, where only the figures without the name of any book occur, they refer to the *śloka* of this particular Upaniṣad.

PUBLISHER

PREFACE TO THE FIRST EDITION

It gladdens our heart to publish the *Kena Upaniṣad* in the present series, soon after the release of the *Īśā Upaniṣad*. This is the sixth Upaniṣad to appear separately in the current series, taking each of them entirely from the author's earlier two-volume edition, *Eight Upaniṣads*. Only two more, the *Kaṭha*, and the *Taittirīya*, remain to come out,* the rest having already been published during the last one year and a half. Like the *Īśā Upaniṣad*, the *Kena* also derives its name from the very first word (केन) of the opening verse of this Upaniṣad. It is also called the *Talavakāropaniṣad*, as it forms a part of the *Talavakāra* or *Jaimini Brāhmaṇa*.

Among the principal Upaniṣads, though it is one of the shorter ones, its spiritual significance is great, because Śrī Śaṅkarācārya considered it necessary to write two commentaries on this text, namely *pada-bhāṣya* and *vākya-bhāṣya*. In this edition, only the former has been translated. In the translation of the commentary, the words quoted from the text by the Ācārya are given in italics. These are followed by commas and the English equivalents. Informative explanatory footnotes have been added wherever necessary.

In the *Kena Upaniṣad*, we get the notion of the ultimate Reality as the origin, ground, and goal of all the manifold manifestation. It speaks of the Reality as the inner Self behind all our conceptions and perceptions, after freeing It from all touch of relativity and finitude. It reveals the spiritual Reality as a *given* fact of experience—*pratibodha viditaṁ matam.* It contains the illuminating story of Umā (Haimavatī) imparting spiritual knowledge to the gods, who thought in a moment of self-conceit and self-forgetfulness that they were all-powerful. Their eyes were opened by right knowledge.

Finally this Upaniṣad lays great stress on the unique opportunity given to human birth in the spiritual evolution and unfoldment of the soul. Further, it emphatically declares that Self-realization, is to be had in this very life, and warns that, if we do not attain it here and now, 'then there is great destruction'.

Such is the immense value of this Upaniṣad. It is our privilege, we consider, to place this book in the hands of all earnest seekers of the Upaniṣadic thought who wish to benefit by its study.

Mayavati — PUBLISHER
9 January 1980

* The *Kaṭha Upaniṣad* was later published in February 1980 and the *Taittirīya* in September 1980. —P.

KEY TO TRANSLITERATION AND PRONUNCIATION

		Sounds like			Sounds like
अ	a	o in s*o*n	ड	ḍ	d
आ	ā	a in m*a*ster	ढ	ḍh	dh in go*dh*ood
इ	i	i in *i*f	ण	ṇ	n in u*n*der
ई	ī	ee in f*ee*l	त	t	French t
उ	u	u in f*u*ll	थ	th	th in *th*umb
ऊ	ū	oo in b*oo*t	द	d	th in *th*en
ऋ	ṛ	somewhat between r and ri	ध	dh	theh in brea*the* *h*ere
ए	e	a in ev*a*de	न	n	n
ऐ	ai	y in m*y*	प	p	p
ओ	o	o in *o*ver	फ	ph	ph in loo*p-h*ole
औ	au	ow in n*ow*	ब	b	b
क	k	k	भ	bh	bh in a*bh*or
ख	kh	ckh in blo*ckh*ead	म	m	m
ग	g	g (hard)	य	y	y
घ	gh	gh in lo*g-h*ut	र	r	r
ङ	ṅ	ng	ल	l	l
च	c	ch (not k)	व	v	v in a*v*ert
छ	ch	chh in cat*ch h*im	श	ś	sh
ज	j	j	ष	ṣ	sh in *sh*ow
झ	jh	dgeh in he*dgeh*og	स	s	s
ञ	ñ	n (somewhat)	ह	h	h
ट	ṭ	t	ं	ṁ	m in hu*m*
ठ	ṭh	th in an*t-h*ill	ः	ḥ	half h in hu*h*!

LIST OF ABBREVIATIONS

Ā.G.	...	Ānanda Giri
Ai	...	Aitareya Upaniṣad
Ai.Ā.	...	Aitareya Āraṇyaka
Bṛ.	...	Bṛhadāraṇyaka Upaniṣad
Ch.	...	Chāndogya Upaniṣad
G.	...	Bhagavad Gītā
Īś.	...	Īśā Upaniṣad
Ka.	...	Kaṭha Upaniṣad
Kai.	...	Kaivalya Upaniṣad
Mā.	...	Māṇḍūkya Upaniṣad
Mbh.	...	Mahābhārata
Mu.	...	Muṇḍaka Upaniṣad
Muk.	...	Muktika Upaniṣad
Nṛ.	...	Nṛsiṁha-pūrva-tāpanī Upaniṣad
Pr.	...	Praśṇa Upaniṣad
Śv.	...	Śvetāśvatara Upaniṣad
Tai.	...	Taittirīya Upaniṣad
Tai B.	...	Taittirīya Brāhmaṇa
V.Sm.	...	Viṣnu Smṛti

KENA UPANIṢAD

ॐ आप्यायन्तु ममाङ्गानि वाक्प्राणश्चक्षुः श्रोत्रमथो बल-
मिन्द्रियाणि च सर्वाणि। सर्वं ब्रह्मौपनिषदं माऽहं ब्रह्म निराकुर्यां
मा मा ब्रह्म निराकरोदनिराकरणमस्त्वनिराकरणं मेऽस्तु।
तदात्मनि निरते य उपनिषत्सु धर्मास्ते मयि सन्तु ते मयि
सन्तु।

ॐ शान्तिः शान्तिः शान्तिः ॥

May my limbs, speech, vital force, eyes, ears, as also strength and all the organs, become well developed. Everything is the Brahman revealed in the Upaniṣads. May I not deny Brahman; may not Brahman deny me. Let there be no spurning (of me by Brahman), let there be no rejection (of Brahman) by me. May all the virtues that are (spoken of) in the Upaniṣads repose in me who am engaged in the pursuit of the Self; may they repose in me.

Om! Peace! Peace! Peace!

KENA UPANIṢAD

PART I

Introduction: Since the Upaniṣad commencing with *Keneṣitam* and revealing the supreme Brahman has to be spoken of, the ninth chapter[1] begins. Earlier than this, rites have been exhaustively dealt with, and the (different) meditations on the vital force as the basis of rites, as also the meditations on the (various) *Sāmas*[2], forming parts of rites, have been spoken of. After that is stated the meditation on the *Gāyatra Sāma*, (thought of as the vital force), which ends with a succession of teachers and pupils and which relates to effects of action. If all these rites and meditations, as enjoined, are properly observed, they become the cause of purification of the mind of one who is free from desires and longs for emancipation. But in the case of one who cherishes desires and has no enlightenment (i.e. meditation on or knowledge of gods), the rites by themselves, as enjoined in the Vedas and Smṛtis, become the cause for the attainment of the Southern Path and for return to this world. But through activity prompted by natural impulses that are repugnant to the scriptures, there will be degradation into lower beings ranging from beasts to the motionless ones (trees etc.) in accordance with the

[1] The Kena Upaniṣad forms part of the Upaniṣad Brāhmaṇa of the Talavakāra branch of the Sāma-Veda.

[2] A *Sāma* song is divided into parts — five or seven. This *Sāma* as also each of its parts has to be thought of variously. For such meditation see Ch. I. and II.

Vedic text. '(If one does not perform rites or meditation), then one does not proceed by either of these Paths (Northern or Southern). They become these little creatures (mosquitoes etc.) that are constantly subject to birth and death following the (divine) order "Be born and die." This is the third state' (Ch.V. x.8); and in accordance with the words of the other text: 'Three kinds of beings[1] followed a course that deviates (from these Northern and Southern Paths)'[2] (Ai. Ā. II. i. 1. 4). The longing for the knowledge of the indwelling Self arises only in that desireless man of pure mind who has renounced all transitory, external means and ends by virtue of the emergence of a special kind of tendency (in his mind) created by works done in this life or in previous ones. This fact is being shown in the form of questions and answers by the Vedic text beginning with *Keneṣitam*. In the Kaṭha Upaniṣad, too, it is said, 'The self-existent Lord destroyed the outgoing senses; therefore one sees the outer things and not the Self within. A rare discriminating man, desiring immortality, turns his eyes away and then sees the indwelling Self' (Ka. II. i. 1) etc. And in the (Muṇḍaka) Upaniṣad of the Atharva-Veda it is said, 'Having examined the worlds attainable by work thus: "The unproduced (everlasting emancipation) is not to be produced by work", the Brāhmaṇa should resort to renunciation. In order to know that Reality fully, he must go, with sacrificial faggots in hand, only to a teacher versed in the Vedas

[1] Born from the womb, egg, or earth.

[2] And thereby they tread a path of sorrow.

and is established in Brahman' (Mu. I. ii. 12). In this way alone, does a man of detachment acquire the competence to hear, meditate on, and realize the knowledge of the indwelling Self, and not otherwise. Besides, as a result of this realization of the indwelling Self as Brahman, there comes the total cessation of ignorance which is the seed of bondage and the cause of the emergence of desire and activity, in accordance with the verse: 'What sorrow and what delusion can there be for that seer of oneness?' (Īś.7); and also in accordance with the Vedic texts: 'The knower of the Self transcends sorrow' (Ch.VII.1.3); 'When the One that is both cause and effect is realized the knot of the heart (of the seer) gets untied, all (his) doubts are resolved, and all *karma* is consumed' (Mu. II. ii. 8) etc.

Objection: May it not be argued that this result can be attained even from knowledge[1] coupled with rites and duties?

Answer: No, because in the Vājasaneyaka (Bṛhadāraṇyaka) Upaniṣad that (combination of rites and meditation) has been spoken of as the cause of a different result. Starting with the text, 'Let me have a wife' (Bṛ. I. iv. 17), the Vājasaneyaka shows in the text, 'This world of man is to be won through the son alone, and by no other rite; the world of the Manes through rites; and the world of the gods through

[1] The word *jñāna* occurs in two senses: (i) Vedāntic knowledge and (ii) knowledge about gods or meditation on them. *Jñāna* in the second sense can be combined with rites and duties, but not Vedāntic *jñāna*.

meditation' (Bṛ.I.v.16), how rites and duties lead to the attainment of the three worlds that are different from the Self. And there (in that Upaniṣad itself), again, the reason for embracing renunciation is adduced thus: 'What shall we achieve through children, we to whom the Self we have attained is the goal?' (Bṛ. IV. iv. 22). The explanation of that reason is this: What shall we do with progeny, rites, and meditation combined with rites, which are the means for the attainment of worlds other than that of the Self, and are the causes for the attainment of the three worlds of men, Manes, and gods? Nor are the three worlds—transitory and attainable by means as they are—desirable to us, to whom is desirable the world that is natural, 'birthless, undecaying, immortal, fearless' (Bṛ. IV. v. 25), that 'neither increases nor decreases through work' (Bṛ. IV. iv. 23), and is eternal. And being eternal, it is not to be secured by any means other than the cessation of ignorance. Hence the only duty is to renounce all desires after the realization of the unity of the indwelling Self and Brahman. Besides, the knowledge of the identity of the indwelling Self and Brahman militates against its co-existence with work, because the realization of the identity of the Self and Brahman, which eradicates all dual ideas, cannot reasonably coexist with work which presupposes the ideas of the difference of agent and results; for the object (of knowledge) being the deciding factor, the realization of Brahman is not determined by human effort.[1]

[1] 'An object of injunction is that which has to be achieved by effort consequent on the injunction. Knowledge is not of that kind'

Therefore this desire to know the indwelling Self, in the case of a man who has renounced all seen and unseen results attainable by external means, is being shown by the Vedic text beginning with *Keneṣitam*. But the object (of the inquiry) being subtle, the presentation in the form of questions and answers of the student and teacher leads to easy comprehension; and it is also shown that the object is not realizable through mere dialectics. Moreover, in accordance with the Vedic text, 'This wisdom is not to be attained through dialectics' (Ka. I. ii. 9), and the obligation about taking a teacher implied in the Vedic and Smṛti texts, 'One who has a teacher acquires knowledge' (Ch. VI. xiv. 2), 'Such knowledge alone as is acquired from a teacher becomes the best'[1] (Ch. IV. ix. 3). 'Learn that through obeisance' (G. IV. 34), it can be imagined that someone, having found no refuge in anything other than the indwelling Self, and having a longing for the fearless, eternal, auspicious, and unshakable (Brahman), approached a teacher who is established in Brahman, and asked:

ॐ केनेषितं पतति प्रेषितं मनः
केन प्राणः प्रथमः प्रैति युक्तः।
केनेषितां वाचमिमां वदन्ति
चक्षुः श्रोत्रं क उ देवो युनक्ति ॥१॥

—Ā.G. The object is the determining factor as regards the content of any valid knowledge. Neither injunction nor any accessory has any effect here.

[1] 'Leads to the acquisition of the best result.'—Ā.G.

1. Willed by whom does the directed mind go towards its object? Being directed by whom does the vital force that precedes all, proceed (towards its duty)? By whom is this speech willed that people utter? Who is the effulgent being who directs the eyes and the ears?

Kena, by what agent; being *iṣitam*, willed, directed; *manaḥ*, the mind; *patati*, goes, goes towards its own object — this is the construction. Since the root *iṣ* cannot be taken here to imply either repetition or going;[1] it must be understood that the present form of the root is in its sense of desiring. The form in which the suffix *it* is used in the word *iṣitam* is a Vedic licence[2]. *Preṣitam* is a form of the same root, with *pra* prefixed to it, in the sense of directing. If the word *preṣitam* alone were used (without *iṣitam*) there would arise such an inquiry about the particular kind of director and the direction as: 'By what particular director? And how is the direction?' But the attribute *iṣitam* being there, both the questions are set at rest, because thereby is ascertained a special meaning, viz 'directed (*preṣitam*) through whose mere will?'[3]

Objection: If this be the meaning intended, the purpose is served by the expression *willed by* alone, and the expression *directed* need not be used. Moreover, since it is reasonable that an additional word should imply an additional meaning, it is proper to under-

[1] 'Since the intention here is not to make the mind an object of the concept of either repeated occurrence or going, and since the desire is for knowing some special director of the mind.' — Ā.G.

[2] The correct form should have been '*eṣitam*.' — Ā.G.

[3] 'By mere presence that involves no effort.' — Ā.G.

stand some special sense as: 'By what is it directed—by will, act, or speech?'

Answer: This cannot be so because of the trend of the question. For the reasonable conclusion derived from the trend (of the question) is that the inquiry is made by a man who has become disgusted with the ephemeral works and their results, such as the assemblage of the body, senses, etc., and seeks to know something other than these, which is unchangeable and eternal. If it were not so, the question would be surely meaningless, since the directorship of the group of body etc. (over the mind) through will, word, and act is a familiar fact.

Objection: Even so, the sense of the word *directed* is not certainly brought out.

Answer: No, since the word *directed* can reasonably convey a special sense, viz that it is the question of a man in doubt. Both the adjectives *iṣitam* (willed) and *preṣitam* (directed), in the sentence *willed by whom the directed mind goes*, are justifiable as implying: 'Does the directorship belong to the aggregate of body and senses, which is a well-known fact; or does the directorship through mere will, over the mind etc., belong to some independent entity which is different from the aggregate?'

Objection: Is it not a well-known fact that the mind is free and goes independently to its own object? How can the question arise with regard to that matter?

The *answer* is this: If the mind were independent in engaging and disengaging itself, then nobody would have contemplated any evil. And yet the mind, though conscious of consequences, wills evil; and though dissuaded, it does engage in deeds of intensely sorrowful result. Hence the question, *keneṣitam patati* etc., is appropriate.

Kena, by whom; *prāṇaḥ*, the vital force; being *yuktaḥ*, engaged, directed; *praiti*, goes, towards its own activity? *Prathamaḥ*, first, should be an adjective of the vital force, for the activities of all the organs are preceded by it. *Imām vācam*, this speech, consisting of words; which ordinary people *vadanti*, utter; *kena iṣitam*, by whom is it willed (during that utterance)? Similarly, *kaḥ u devaḥ*, which effulgent being; *yunakti*, engages, directs towards their respective objects; *cakṣuḥ śrotram*, the eyes and the ears?

To the worthy disciple who had asked thus, the teacher said, 'Hear what you have asked for in the question, "Who is that effulgent being who is the director of the mind and other organs towards their own objects, and how does he direct?"'

श्रोत्रस्य श्रोत्रं मनसो मनो यद्
वाचो ह वाचं स उ प्राणस्य प्राणः ।
चक्षुषश्चक्षुरतिमुच्य धीराः
प्रेत्यास्माल्लोकादमृता भवन्ति ॥२॥

2. Since He is the Ear of the ear, the Mind of the mind, the Speech of speech, the Life of life, and the Eye of the eye, therefore the intelligent men after giving up (self-identification with the senses) and renouncing this world, become immortal.

Śrotrasya śrotram, the Ear of the ear. The *śrotram*

is that by which one hears, the instrument for the hearing of sound, the organ of hearing which reveals words. He about whom you put the question, 'Who is the effulgent being who directs the eyes and the ears?'—is the Ear of the ear.

Objection: Is it not incongruous to answer, 'He is the Ear of the ear', when the reply should have been, 'So-and-so, with such and such attributes, directs the ears etc.'?

Answer: This is no fault, because His distinction cannot be ascertained otherwise. If the director of the ears etc. could be known as possessed of His own activity, independently of the activities of the ears etc. just as it is in the case of the wielder of sickle etc., then this answer would be incongruous. But as a matter of fact, no director of ears etc., possessed of his own activity, is apprehended here like a mower possessed of a sickle etc. But He can be known (as existing unmixed with the ear etc.) from the logical necessity that such activities as deliberation, volition, determination, of those very composite things, viz the ear etc., must be meant for some one's benefit. Just as in the case of a house, so also (in this case) there does exist some one, standing outside the conglomeration of ears etc., by whose necessity is impelled the group of ears etc. Thus from the fact that composite things exist for the need of some one else, a director of the ears etc. can be known (i.e., inferred).[1]

[1] 'Ears etc. are subsidiary to some one different from themselves, for they are composite things, like a house etc.—by this inference the master of the ears etc. can be known. If he, too, should be a part of the combination, then he will be insentient like the house etc. Then we shall have to imagine another master for him, and

Hence the reply, 'He is the Ear of the ear', etc. is quite appropriate.

Objection: What, again, can there be in the significance here of the expression, 'The Ear of the ear' etc.? For just as a light has no need for another light, so in this context the ear can have no need for another ear.

Answer: There is no such fault. The significance here of the expression is this: The ear, to wit, is seen to be able to reveal its own object. This ability of the ear to reveal its own object is possible only when the eternal non-composite, all-pervading light of the Self is there, but not otherwise. Hence the expression, 'Ear of the ear' etc. is justifiable. To the same effect there are other Vedic texts: 'It is through the light of the Self that he sits' (Bṛ. IV. iii. 6), 'Through His light all this shines' (Ka. II. ii. 15; Śv. VI. 14; Mu. II. ii. 10), 'Kindled by which light the sun shines' (Tai. B. III. xii. 9.7), etc. And in the Gītā, '(Know that light to be mine), which is in the sun and which illumines the whole universe' (XV. 12), and '(As the one sun illumines the whole universe), so does He who reside in the body, O descendant of Bharata, illumine the whole body' (XIII. 33). So also in the Kaṭha Upaniṣad, 'the eternal among the ephemeral, the the consciousness among all that is conscious' (II. ii. 13). It is a commonly accepted belief that the ears etc. constitute the Self of all, and that these are conscious. This is being refuted here. There does exist

so also a third for this. Thus to avoid an infinite regress, a Consciousness that is not a part of the combination is apprehended.' —Ā.G.

something which is known to the intellect of the men of realization, which dwells in the inmost recesses of all, which is changeless, undecaying, immortal, fearless, and unborn, and which is the Ear etc., of even the ear etc., i.e. the source of their capacity to act. Thus the answer and significance of the words can certainly be justified.

Similarly, *manasaḥ*, of the mind, of the internal organ; (He is) the *manaḥ*, Mind; because the internal organ is not able to perform its own functions—thinking, determination, etc.—unless it is illumined by the light of consciousness. Therefore He is the Mind of the mind, too. Here the mind and the intellect are jointly mentioned by the word *manaḥ* (mind). *Yad vāco ha vācam*: the word *yat*, used in the sense of because, is connected with all such words as *śrotra* (ear) in this way: because He is the Ear of the ear, because He is the Mind of the mind, and so on. The objective case in *vāco ha vācam* is to be changed into the nominative in consonance with the expression *prāṇasya prāṇaḥ* (the Life of life).

Objection: In conformity with *vāco ha vācam*, why should not the conversion be into the objective case thus: *prāṇasya prāṇam*?

Answer: No, for it is reasonable to conform to the majority. So in consonance with the two words, (*saḥ* and *prāṇaḥ*), in *saḥ u prāṇasya prāṇaḥ* (where they are in the nominative case), the implication of the word *vācam* is *vāk*, for thus is the reasonable conformity with the majority maintained. Moreover, a thing asked about should properly be denoted in the first (nominative) case. He, of whom you ask, and who is the

Life of *prāṇa*—of that particular function called life, by Him, indeed, is ensured the capacity of the vital force to discharge its functions of sustaining life, and this is because there can be no sustaining of life by anything that is not presided over by the Self, in accordance with the Vedic texts: 'Who, indeed, will inhale, and who will exhale, if this Bliss (Brahman) be not there in the supreme Space (within the heart)?' (Tai. II. vii. 1), 'Who pushes the *prāṇa* upward and impels the *apāna* inward' (Ka. II. ii. 3), etc. Here, too, it will be said, 'That which man does not smell with *prāṇa* (the organ of smell), but that by which *prāṇa* is impelled, know that to be Brahman' (1.9).

Objection: Is it not proper to understand *prāṇa* as the sense of smelling (and not life)[1] in a context which deals with the senses—ears etc.?

Answer: This is true. But the text considers that by the mention of *prāṇa* (meaning the vital force) the sense of smell is referred to *ipso facto*. The meaning intended in the context is this: That for whose purpose occurs the activity of all the (motor and sensory) organs is Brahman.

So also He is the *cakṣuṣaḥ cakṣuḥ*, the Eye of the eye; the capacity to perceive colour that the eye, the organ of sight, possesses is merely by virtue of its being presided over by the consciousness of the Self. Hence He is the Eye of the eye. Since a questioner's desire is to know the thing he asks for, the expression, 'having known' has to be supplied thus: 'Having known Brahman, as the Ear etc. of the ear etc., as indicated

[1] The word *prāṇa* is used in different senses in different contexts. It may mean vital force, exhaling, sense of smell, etc.

before.' This (addition) is also necessary, because the result is stated thus, 'They become immortal' (II. 5), and because immortality is attained through realization. From the fact that a man becomes free after getting realization, it follows (that he becomes immortal) by giving up, (through the strength of knowledge), the group of organs beginning with the ear; that is to say, since by identifying the Self with the ear etc. a man becomes conditioned by these and takes birth, dies, and transmigrates, therefore having realized, as one's Self, the Brahman that is defined as the 'Ear of the ear' etc., and *atimucya*, giving up self-identification with the ear etc.—(he becomes immortal). Those who give up self-identification with the ear etc. are the *dhīrāḥ*, intelligent, because the self-identification with the ear etc. cannot be given up unless one is endowed with uncommon intellect. *Pretya*, desisting; *asmāt lokāt*, from this world of empirical dealings involving ideas of 'I and mine' with regard to sons, friends, wives, and relatives; i.e. having renounced all desires; (they) *bhavanti*, become; *amṛtāḥ*, immortal, immune from death. This is in accordance with the Vedic texts: 'Not by work, not by progeny, not by wealth, but by renunciation some (rare ones) attained immortality' (Kai. 1.2), 'The self-existent Lord destroyed the outgoing senses; hence one perceives the external things and not the Self within. A rare, discriminating man, longing for immortality, turns his eyes away and then sees the indwelling Self' (Ka. II. i. 1), 'When all desires that cling to one's heart fall off, . . . then one attains Brahman here' (Ka. II. iii. 14), etc. Or, renunciation of desires being implied in the expression *atimucya* (giving up) itself, *asmāt lokāt pretya* means separating from this body, dying.

न तत्र चक्षुर्गच्छति न वाग्गच्छति नो मनः।
न विद्मो न विजानीमो यथैतदनुशिष्यात् ॥३॥

3. The eye does not go there, nor speech, nor mind. We do not know (Brahman to be such and such); hence we are not aware of any process of instructing about It.

Since Brahman, as the Ear etc. of the ear etc., is the Self of those organs, therefore, *tatra*, there, to that Brahman; *cakṣuḥ*, the eye; *na gacchati*, does not go; for it is not possible to go to oneself. Similarly *na vāk gacchati*, speech does not go. When a word, as expressed by the organ of speech, reveals its own idea, speech is said to go to its object. But Brahman is the Self of that word, as also of the organ that utters it; therefore speech does not go. Just as fire, which burns and illumines, does not burn or illumine itself, similarly is this so. *No manaḥ*, nor the mind. Though the mind thinks and determines other things, it does not think or determine itself; for of it, too, Brahman is the Self. A thing is cognized only by the mind and the senses. As Brahman is not an object of perception to these, therefore, *na vidmaḥ*, we do not know, 'That Brahman is of this kind'. Hence *na vijānīmaḥ*, we are not aware of; *yathā*, the process by which; *etat*, this Brahman; *anuśiṣyāt*, should be taught, instructed to a disciple—this is the significance. For, a thing that is perceived by the senses can be taught to another through categories denoting class, quality, and action. Brahman is not possessed of these categories, viz class etc.; hence it is very difficult to convince the disciples about It through instruction. In this way the Upaniṣad shows the necessity of putting forth great effort in the matter of imparting instruction and comprehending its meaning.

The contingency of the total denial of any process of instruction having arisen from the text, 'We do not know Brahman, and hence we are not aware of any process of instructing about It', an exception to this is being stated in the next verse. True it is that one cannot impart knowledge about the Highest with the help of such means of valid knowledge as the evidence of the senses; but the knowledge can be produced with the help of traditional authority. Therefore traditional authority[1] is being quoted for the sake of imparting instruction about It:

अन्यदेव तद्विदितादथो अविदितादधि।
इतिशुश्रुम पूर्वेषां ये नस्तद्व्याचचक्षिरे ॥४॥

4. 'That (Brahman) is surely different from the known; and again, It is above the unknown'—such was (the utterance) we heard of the ancient (teachers) who explained It to us.

[1] The word used by Śaṅkara is *āgama*, which literally means traditional knowledge which has come down through the line of teachers and pupils. By quoting traditional teaching one does not expose one-self to the charge of speaking about something that defies speech.

Anyat eva, different indeed; is *tat*, that which is the topic under discussion and which has been spoken of as the Ear etc., of the ear etc., and as beyond their reach. It is, indeed, different from the known. The known is very much within the grasp of the act of knowing, that which is the object of the verb, 'to know'. Inasmuch as everything is known somewhere by somebody, all that is manifested is certainly known. The idea is that, It (Brahman) is different from that. Lest, in that case, It should be unknown, the text says, (It is,) *atho*, again; different *aviditāt*, from the unknown, from what is opposed to the known, from that which consists of the unmanifested ignorance, which is the seed of the manifested. The word *adhi*, used in the sense of 'above', means 'different' by a figure of speech; for it is well-known that anything that exists above another is different from that other. Whatever is known is limited, mortal, and full of misery; and hence it is to be rejected. So when it is said that Brahman is different from the known it amounts to asserting that It is not to be rejected. Similarly, when it is affirmed that It is different from the unknown, it amounts to saying that It is not a thing to be obtained. It is for the sake of getting an effect, indeed, that somebody different from it acquires some other thing to serve as a cause. For this reason, too, nothing different (from the Self) need be acquired to serve any purpose distinct from the knower (Self). Thus the statement, that Brahman is different from the known and the unknown, having amounted to Brahman being denied as an object to be acquired or rejected, the desire of the disciple to know Brahman (objectively) comes to an end, for Brahman is non-different from the Self. (Or, according to a different reading — the desire of the disciple to know a Brahman different from the Self, comes to an end).[1] For nothing other than one's own Self can possibly be different from the known and the unknown. Thus it follows that the meaning of the sentence is that the Self is Brahman. And this also follows from such Vedic texts as: 'This Self is Brahman' (Mā. 2; Bṛ. II. v. 19, IV. iv. 5), 'that Self which is untouched by sin' (Ch. VIII. vii. 1), 'the Brahman that is immediate and direct — the Self that is within all' (Bṛ. III. iv. 1), etc. In this way, the text, 'Thus we heard' etc., states how through a succession of preceptors and disciples, was derived the purport of the sentence which establishes as Brahman that Self of all which is devoid of all distinguishing features, and is the light of pure consciousness. Moreover, Brahman is to be known only through such a traditional instruction of preceptors and not through argumentation, nor by study (or exposition), intelligence, great learning, austerity, sacrifices, etc. — *iti*, such (was what); *śuśruma*, we heard; *pūrveṣām*, of the ancient teachers; the teachers *ye*, who; *vyācacakṣire*, explained, taught clearly; *naḥ*, to us; *tat*, that Brahman.

The idea that the Self is Brahman having been established through the sentence, 'That is surely different from the known, and again, that is above the unknown', the hearer has this doubt: 'How can

[1] The expression concerned is *svātmano'nanyatvāt brahmaviṣayā jijñāsā*, or *svātmano'nyabrahmaviṣayā jijñāsā*.

the Self be Brahman? For the Self is familiarly known to be that which is entitled to undertake rites and meditation and which, being subject to birth and death, seeks to attain either the gods headed by Brahmā (Creator) or heaven by undertaking the practice of rites or meditation. Therefore some adorable being other than that (Self), e.g. Viṣṇu, Īśvara (Siva), Indra, or Prāṇa (vital force or Hiraṇyagarbha) may well be Brahman, but not so the Self; for this is opposed to common sense. Just as other logicians say that the Self is different from the Lord, so also the ritualists worship other gods saying, "Sacrifice to that one", "Sacrifice to that one". Therefore it is reasonable that, that should be Brahman which is known and adorable; and the worshipper should be one who is different from this.' Having noticed this doubt either from the looks or the words of the disciple, the teacher said, 'Don't be in doubt thus;'—

यद्वाचाऽनभ्युदितं येन वागभ्युद्यते ।
तदेव ब्रह्म त्वं विद्धि नेदं यदिदमुपासते ॥५॥

5. That which is not uttered by speech, that by which speech is revealed, know that alone to be Brahman, and not what people worship as an object.

Yat, that—whose essence consists of Consciousness alone—, which; (is not uttered) *vācā*, by speech—. *Vāk* (speech) is the organ which, clinging to the eight localities, viz the root of the tongue etc.[1], and being

[1] Chest, throat, head, root of the tongue, teeth, nose, lips, and palate.

presided over by (the god of) Fire, expresses the letters. The letters, too, as limited in their number and as subject to a certain sequence, in conformity with the meaning intended to be conveyed, are also called *vāk.*[1] Thus also the sound expressible by them, which is the *pada* (*sphoṭa*),[2] is called *vāk.* This is in accordance with the Vedic text: 'The letter *a*, indeed, is all speech.[3] And that speech, being manifested as the *sparśa* letters, the *antaḥstha* letters (semi-vowels), and *uṣma* letters (aspirates),[4] becomes many and multifarious' (Ai. Ā. II. iii. 7. 13). (*Yat*, that which) is *anabhyuditam*, not expressed, not uttered; *vācā*, by *vāk*, by speech, which has these modifications, viz regulated (material, *Ṛk*), non-regulated (prose *Yajuḥ*), musical (*Sāma*), true, and false—by that *vāk* which becomes defined as words and to which the organ of speech is subordinate;[5] *yena*, that by which—that Brahman, the

[1] The word *gau* (cow), for instance, consists of the letter *g* and *au* which are fixed as regards their sequence so as to be able to express the meaning cow. This is the view of the Mīmāṁsaka school.

[2] This is the view of the Sphoṭavādī grammarians. '*Sphoṭa* is derived from the root *sphuṭ* in the sense of *that which is manifested* by letters, i.e. that which imparts definite knowledge of word (*pada*), sentence, etc. Their idea is that this (*pada-*) *sphoṭa* has to be admitted since a unified idea (conveyed by the word) cannot be contingent on a multiplicity of letters.'—Ā.G.

[3] 'That Power of Consciousness is *vāk* which is indicated by *Om*, in which *a* predominates. (*Om* is a combination of *a*, *u*, *m*), and this *Om* is called *sphoṭa*,'—Ā.G.

[4] *Sparśa*—25 consonants from *ka* to *ma*; *antaḥstha*—*y*, *r. l*, *v*; *uṣma*—*ś*, *ṣ*, *s*, *h*.

[5] 'The power of speech that human beings have, is established in sounds and letters, for it is expressed by these.'

light of Consciousness, by which—; *vāk*, speech, together with its organs; *abhyudyate*, is uttered, is expressed, that is to say, is used in relation to the desired meaning—. That which has been spoken of here as 'the Speech of speech' (1.2), and as 'When It speaks, It is called the organ of speech' (Bṛ. I. iv. 7), and 'He who controls the organ of speech from within' (Bṛ. III. vii. 17), etc., in the Bṛhadāraṇyaka Upaniṣad, and about whom the question has been raised thus, 'The (power of) speech that is found in men, is established in sounds. Does any Brāhmaṇa know it?', and the answer has been given by saying, 'That by which one speaks in dream is speech'—that eternal power of speech which a speaker has is *vāk* which is in essence, the light of Consciousness. And this follows from the Vedic text, 'For the speaker's power of speech can never be lost' (Bṛ. IV. iii. 26). *Tat eva*, that indeed, that Self in its true nature; *tvam*, you; *viddhi*, know; as *brahma*, Brahman—(so called) because of its extensity (or unsurpassability)—that which is all-surpassing and is called Bhūmā, great (Ch. VII. xxiii. 1). The significance of the word *eva* is this: Know the Self alone to be the unconditioned Brahman after eradicating all such adjuncts as speech because of which there occur such empirical expressions, with regard to the transcendental, unconditioned, unsurpassable, and equipoised Brahman, as 'It is the Speech of speech', 'the Eye of the eye', 'the Ear of the ear', 'the Mind of the mind', the agent, the enjoyer, the knower, the controller, governor. 'Consciousness, Bliss, Brahman' (Bṛ. III. ix. 28.7), etc. *Na idam*, this is not; *brahma*, Brahman; *yat*, which; people *upāsate*, meditate on; as *idam*, this, (as a limited object) possessed of distinctions created by limiting adjuncts—as a non-Self, e.g. God, etc. Although in the sentence, 'know that alone to be Brahman', it has already been stated that the non-Self is not Brahman, still with a view to enunciating an explicit rule (that leaves no scope for option) the idea is repeated in the sentence, 'This is not Brahman'; or this may be with a view to excluding the identification of Brahman with what is not Brahman.[1]

यन्मनसा न मनुते येनाहुर्मनो मतम् ।
तदेव ब्रह्म त्वं विद्धि नेदं यदिदमुपासते ॥६॥

6. That which man does not comprehend with the mind, that by which, they say, the mind is encompassed, know that to be Brahman and not what people worship as an object.

Manas means the internal organs, mind and intellect being taken as one entity. The word *manas*, derived from the root *man* in the sense of that by which one thinks, is common to all organs, since it embraces all objects. In accordance with the Vedic text, 'Desire, deliberation, doubt, faith, want of faith, steadiness, unsteadiness, shame, intelligence, and fear—all these are but the mind' (Bṛ. I. v. 3), mind is that which has desire etc. as its functions. *Yat*, that—the light of

[1] In Mīmāṁsā philosophy *Niyama-vidhi* pins one down to one thing only when alternatives are possible. Here the possibilities are, thinking of both Brahman and non-Brahman as Brahman. And the rule fixes us to the pursuit of Brahman only. *Parisaṅkhyā-vidhi* merely excludes something—here the thought of non-Brahman as Brahman. So the text may be interpreted from either point of view.

Consciousness illumining the mind—, which; one *na manute*, does not think nor determine, with that mind, because It rules the mind by virtue of being the enlightener of the mind—. Since the Self, indeed, constitutes the essence of everything, therefore the mind cannot act with regard to its own Self. The mind can think only when it is illumined by the light of Consciousness within. That Brahman, *yena*, by which; —they, the knowers of Brahman; *āhuḥ*, say—; *manas*, the mind, together with its modes; *matam*, is thought of, encompassed—. Therefore *viddhi*, know, *tat eva*, that very one, the Self of the mind, the internal illuminator, as Brahman. *Na idam*, etc. is to be understood as before.

यच्चक्षुषा न पश्यति येन चक्षूंषि पश्यति ।
तदेव ब्रह्म त्वं विद्धि नेदं यदिदमुपासते ॥७॥

7. That which man does not see with the eye, that by which man perceives the activities of the eye, know that alone to be Brahman and not what people worship as an object.

Yat, that which; *cakṣuṣā*, with the eye, associated with the functions of the internal organ; *na paśyati*, (a man) does not see, does not make an object of perception; *yena*, that by which; man *paśyati*, sees, perceives, encompasses, through the light of Consciousness; *cakṣūṁṣi*, the activities of the eye—diversified in accordance with the modes of the internal organ—. *Tat eva*, etc., as before.

यच्छ्रोत्रेण न शृणोति येन श्रोत्रमिदं श्रुतम् ।
तदेव ब्रह्म त्वं विद्धि नेदं यदिदमुपासते ॥८॥

8. That which man does not hear with the ear, that by which man knows this ear, know that to be Brahman and not this that people worship as an object.

Yat śrotreṇa na śṛṇoti, that which man does not hear with the ear, that is presided over by the deity of the quarters, that is produced from *ākāśa*, and that is connected with the activity of the mind; *yena*, that by which, by which light of Consciousness; *idam śrotram śrutam*, this well-known ear is encompassed—. *Tat eva*, etc., as before.

यत्प्राणेन न प्राणिति येन प्राणः प्रणीयते।
तदेव ब्रह्म त्वं विद्धि नेदं यदिदमुपासते ॥९॥

इति केनोपनिषदि प्रथमः खण्डः ॥

9. That which man does not smell with the organ of smell, that by which the organ of smell is impelled, know that to be Brahman and not what people worship as an object.

Prāṇena, by the organ of smell, produced from earth, existing in the nostrils, and associated with the activities of the internal organ and the vital force; *yat*, that which; man *na prāṇiti*, does not smell, does not comprehend like smell; *yena*, that light of the Self by which; *prāṇaḥ*, the organ of smell—being illumined as an object; *praṇīyate*, is impelled—towards its own object—. All the rest, *tat eva* etc., is just like what has gone before.

PART II

यदि मन्यसे सुवेदेति दहरमेवापि
नूनं त्वं वेत्थ ब्रह्मणो रूपम् ।
यदस्य त्वं यदस्य देवेष्वथ नु
मीमाꣳस्यमेव ते मन्ये विदितम् ॥१॥

1. (Teacher): 'If you think, "I have known Brahman well enough", then you have known only the very little expression that It has in the human body and the little expression that It has among the gods. Therefore Brahman is still to be deliberated on by you.' (Disciple): 'I think (Brahman) is known.'

Fearing that the disciple, to whom has been brought home the conviction, 'You are the Self, which is opposed to the acceptable and, the unacceptable, and which is Brahman', may jump to the conclusion, 'I know myself well enough that I, indeed, am Brahman', the teacher, with a view to dispelling that notion of the disciple, says, 'If you think,' etc.

Objection: Is not such a firm conviction as, 'I know well enough', desirable?

Answer: True, a firm conviction is desirable but not such a one as, 'I know It well enough.' That knowable thing alone that falls within the range of cognition can be known thoroughly, just as an inflammable substance becomes consumable to a fire that burns it, but not so the essence itself of the fire. The well-ascertained purport of all the Upaniṣads is that the personal Self of each knower is Brahman. Here, too, the same fact has been established in the form of an answer to questions, in the text beginning with, 'That which is the Ear of the ear' etc. (1.2); and the same has been specifically affirmed in the text, 'That which is not uttered by speech' (I. 5). Besides, the positive conclusion of the (traditional) line of knowers of Brahman has been adduced in the text: 'That is surely different from the known; and again, It is above the unknown' (I. 4). And the topic will be concluded thus: 'It is unknown to those who know well, and known to those who do not know' (II. 3). Hence it is proper to dispel the disciple's notion: 'I know well enough.' For the knower cannot be known by the knower, just as fire cannot be consumed by the consuming fire; and there is no other knower different from Brahman to whom Brahman can become a separate knowable. A separate knower is denied by the Vedic text: 'There is no other knower but this' (Bṛ. III. viii. 11). Therefore the conviction, 'I know Brahman well enough', is certainly false. Hence the teacher has justifiably said, 'If you think,' etc.

Yadi, if perchance; *manyase*, you think; *su veda iti*, 'I know Brahman well enough.' Although the entity may be inscrutable, yet some one who is possessed of real wisdom and who is free from defects, may at some time comprehend It as it was heard of, whereas some one else may not; hence the teacher says with hesitation, 'If you think,' etc. And it has been noticed that when it was declared, ' "The person that is perceived in the eye — is this Self" ', so said he (Prajāpati). "This is immortal, fearless—this is Brahman"' (Ch. VIII. vii. 4), Virocana, though he was a son of Prajāpati, and a scholar, and a king of the demons, still, owing to his natural defects, understood, contrary to what was taught, an opposite object, viz the body, to be the Self. Similarly, Indra, the king of the gods, who could not comprehend when instructed once, twice, and thrice, did, at the fourth stage, when his natural defects had been removed, realize the same Brahman that was spoken of at the very initial stage (Ch. VIII. vii-xii). In ordinary life also it is seen that, of the disciples hearing from the same teacher, some one understands accurately, some one inaccurately, some one contrarily, and some one nothing at all. What more need one speak with regard to (the knowledge of) the real nature of the Self which is beyond the senses? In this matter, indeed, all dialecticians, whether they believe in (the) existence or non-existence (of the Self), have got their misconceptions. Therefore though the statement, 'Brahman has been realized', has been made with firm conviction, still the teacher's apprehensive remark, 'If you think,' etc., is quite appropriate in view of the comprehension being difficult. *Tvam*, you; *vettha*, know; *nūnam*, certainly; *daharam*[1] *rūpam eva api*, the very little from (i.e. expression); *brahmaṇaḥ*, of Brahman.

Objection: Are there many forms of Brahman, great and small, because of which it is said, 'very little form' etc.?

Answer: Quite so. Many, indeed, are the aspects

[1] A different reading is *dabhram*, having the same sense.

of Brahman created by the adjuncts of name and form, but not naturally. From Its own standpoint, forms, together with words are denied thus: 'That which is without sound, touch, form, and destruction; likewise tasteless, eternal and odourless' (Ka.I. iii. 15; Nṛ. 9; Muk.II. 72).

Objection: Is it not a fact that the very attribute by which a thing is determined is its own nature? Therefore that very distinctive feature by which Brahman is defined must be Its nature. Hence it is argued that since consciousness cannot be an attribute of any one of (the elements), earth etc., nor can it be of all of them in their transformation (as body), and as it is not an attribute of either of (the senses such as) the ear etc., or of the internal organ (mind), therefore it is a feature of Brahman; and thus is Brahman defined by consciousness. Thus it has been said, 'Knowledge, Bliss, Brahman' (Bṛ. III. ix. 28. 7), 'Pure intelligence only' (Bṛ. II. iv. 12), 'Brahman is Truth, Knowledge, Infinite' (Tai. II. i. 1), 'Brahman is consciousness' (Ai. V. 3)—thus, too, is the feature of Brahman determined in the Vedic texts.

Answer: Truly this is so. But even so, that aspect is indicated by such words as consciousness, not from the intrinsic point of view, but merely with reference to the limiting adjuncts—mind, body, and senses—, because of Its correspondence with those things, in accordance as the body etc. undergo expansion, contraction, disruption, destruction, etc. But in reality, the conclusion will be: 'unknown to those who know well, and known to those who do not know' (II.3).

The expression, *yat asya*, should be construed with

the preceding expression, *brahmaṇaḥ rūpam* (the aspect of Brahman), (meaning thereby: that form of Brahman which . . .). Not only do you know very little of the expression of that Brahman that is conditioned by the human personality, but the expression of Brahman as conditioned by divine adjuncts, which you *deveṣu vettha*, know among the gods, that too, as known to you, is very little indeed. This is how I think. Whether the expression be in the human personality or whether it be among the gods, it does not become freed from insignificance, since it is conditioned by adjuncts. The purport is that the Brahman, that is free from all distinctions, that is one without a second, and that is known as Bhūmā (great) and eternal, cannot be known as a fully comprehended object. Since this is so, *atha nu*, therefore; *manye*, I think; *te*, for you; even now, Brahman is *mīmāṁsyam eva*, certainly to be deliberated on. The disciple having been told so by the teacher, sat in solitude with his mind concentrated, deliberated on the traditional teaching as imparted by the teacher together with its purport, ascertained it by a process of reasoning, made it a matter of personal experience, approached the teacher, and said 'Now *manye*, I think; (Brahman) is *viditam*, known.'

(Teacher): 'How (is Brahman known to you)?'
(Disciple): 'Listen!' —

नाहं मन्ये सुवेदेति नो न वेदेति वेद च।
यो नस्तद्वेद तद्वेद नो न वेदेति वेद च॥२॥

2. 'I do not think, "I know (Brahman) well enough": (i.e. I consider) "Not that I do not know; I know and I do not know as well." He among us who understands that utterance, "Not that I do not know; I know and I do not know as well", knows that (Brahman).'

Na aham manye suveda iti, I do not think, 'I know Brahman well enough.' Being told (by the teacher), 'Then Brahman is not certainly known by you', (the disciple) replies, '*No na veda iti, veda ca*, not that I do not know Brahman: and I know, too.' From the use of the word *ca*, (and) in the expression *veda ca*, we are to understand, '*Na veda ca*, and I do not know, as well.'

(Teacher): Is it not contradictory (to say), 'I do not think, "I know (Brahman) well enough,",' and 'Not that I do not know; I know and I do not know as well'? If you do not consider, 'I know well enough', then how can you consider, 'I know too'? Again if you consider, 'I do not know', then why do you not consider, 'I know well enough'? Leaving out of consideration doubt and false knowledge, it is a contradiction to say that the very same thing which is known by a man is not known well enough by him. Nor can a restrictive rule be laid down to the effect that Brahman is to be known as an object of doubt or false knowledge. For doubt and false knowledge are, indeed, everywhere known to be the causes of harm.

Though the disciple was thus given a shaking by the teacher, he remained unmoved. Moreover, revealing his own firm conviction in the knowledge of Brahman, he boldly declared with the strength derived from the traditional knowledge as imparted by the teacher in the sentence, 'It is different from the known and is also above the unknown', as also from the strength derived from reasoning and (personal) realization. How (did he declare)? That is being said: '*Yaḥ*, anyone who; *naḥ*, among us, among my co-disciples; *veda*, knows in reality; *tat*, that, that sentence uttered (by me); he *veda*, knows; *tat*, that Brahman.' (Teacher): 'What again is your assertion?' To this he answers: '*No na veda iti veda ca*, not that I do not know; I know and I do not know as well.' With a view to showing his concurrence with the idea of the teacher and counteracting the comprehension of people of dull intellect, the disciple repeated with conviction in another language, viz 'Not that I do not know; I know and I do not know as well', the very same thing which was presented in the sentence, 'It is different from the known and it is above the unknown'; and in doing so, he associated with this his own inference and realization. Thus the exclamation, 'He among us who understands that utterance knows that (Brahman)', becomes justifiable.

Stepping aside from the dialogue between the teacher and the taught, the Upaniṣad, speaking for itself, presents in these words, *yasyāmatam* etc., the whole of the conclusion arrived at through the dialogue:

यस्यामतं तस्य मतं मतं यस्य न वेद सः ।
अविज्ञातं विजानतां विज्ञातमविजानताम् ॥३॥

3. It is known to him to whom It is unknown; he does not know to whom It is known. It is unknown to those who know well, and known to those who do not know.

To that knower of Brahman, *yasya*, to whom; (It is) *amatam*, unknown—whose view, conviction, is that Brahman is not known; *tasya*, to him; *matam*, is known, Brahman is fully known—that is the meaning. Again, *yasya*, he to whom; (It is) *matam*, known—he who has the conviction, 'Brahman is known to me'; *saḥ*, he; *na veda*, does not know, to be sure; he does not know Brahman. The two views of the man of knowledge and the man of ignorance, which are thus presented, are being distinctly affirmed (in the second line), *avijñātam vijānatām* etc. *Avijñātam*, not known; Brahman is in fact unknown to *vijānatām*, to the people who know—that is to say, to those who have fully realized. Brahman is *vijñātam*, known; *avijānatām*, to those who do not know, to those who have not got full realization—that is to say, to those who identify the Self merely with the senses, the mind, and the intellect, but not to those whose intelligence is extremely primitive, (these latter being left out of consideration), for the latter do not have the consciousness, 'Brahman is known by us'. The error involved in the idea, 'Brahman is known to us', is possible for those, however, who, by reason of non-discrimination between Brahman and the limiting adjuncts, and because of their familiarity with the limiting adjuncts such as the intellect, consider the senses, the mind and the intellect as the Self. Hence the incomplete knowledge is presented as a view to be refuted in the text, 'known to those who do not know'. Or the latter half (of the verse viz) *avijñātam* etc., is adduced as a reason (for the first half).[1]

It has been ascertained that Brahman is unknown to those who know. If Brahman be wholly unknown, then there remains no distinction between the ordinary people and the knowers of Brahman. Besides, the statement, 'unknown to those who know', is self-contradictory. How then can Brahman be known adequately? To explain this the Upaniṣad says:

प्रतिबोधविदितं मतममृतत्वं हि विन्दते।
आत्मना विन्दते वीर्यं विद्यया विन्दतेऽमृतम् ॥४॥

4. It (i.e. Brahman) is really known when It is known with (i.e. as the Self of) each state of consciousness, because thereby one gets immortality. (Since) through one's own Self is acquired strength, (therefore) through knowledge is attained immortality.

Pratibodha-viditam, known with reference to each state of intelligence. By the word *bodha* are meant the cognitions acquired through the intellect. The Self, that encompasses all ideas as Its objects, is known

[1] 'Just as in common experience it is well known that to the people, aware of the nature of the mother of pearl, the silver superimposed on it remains unknown (on that mother of pearl), but to the ignorant alone, the superimposed silver is known (as silver), similarly, knowableness being a thing superimposed on Brahman, the men of realization do not consider that Brahman as known.'—Ā.G.

in relation to all these ideas. Being the witness of all cognitions, and by nature nothing but the power of Consciousness, the Self is indicated by the cognitions themselves, in the midst of cognitions, as pervading (all of) them. There is no other door to Its awareness. Therefore when Brahman is known as the innermost Self (i.e. witness) of cognitions, then is It *matam*, known, that is to say, then there is Its complete realization. Only by accepting Brahman as the witness of all cognitions can it be established that It is by nature a witness that is not subject to growth and decay, and is eternal, pure in essence, the Self, unconditioned, and one in all beings,[1] just as it is in the case of *ākāśa* (space), because of the nondifference of its characteristics despite its existence in pots, caves, etc. The purport of that very traditional text, 'It is different from the known, and again It is above the unknown' (I. 4), which is thus clarified, is concluded here. For (in support of this) there is the other Vedic text: 'The Witness of vision, the Hearer of hearing, the Thinker of thought, the Knower of knowledge' (Bṛ. III. iv. 2).

Again, if the explanation of *pratibodhaviditam* be, 'The Self being the agent of the act of knowing, one infers It to be the agent of the action from the fact of the cognitive act itself, just as one knows that to be the wind which moves a tree', then the Self is a substance possessed of the power of knowing, but It

[1] 'Since the reality of my consciousness, by virtue of which I am the witness, exists equally in all, I am not a mere witness in a single body. And since difference, origination, etc. do not inhere in the witness, therefore the non-duality, eternality, etc. of the witness are also established.' — Ā.G.

is not knowledge itself; and as for knowledge, it originates and dies; when knowledge originates, the Self becomes modified by it; and when knowledge dies, the Self becomes nothing but an unmodified substance with its intelligence destroyed. In such a case, one cannot avoid the objection that the Self (thereby) becomes changeable, composed of parts, non-eternal, impure, etc.

As for the (following) view of the school of Kaṇāda, 'Knowledge, arising from the contact of the soul and the mind, inheres in the soul; hence is the soul endowed with knowership. But it is not changeable; it is merely a substance just like a pot in which colour inheres'—since according to this view, too, Brahman is a mere substance without consciousness, it contradicts such Vedic text as, 'Knowledge, Bliss, Brahman' (Bṛ. III. ix. 28.7), 'Brahman is Consciousness' (Ai. V. 3). And as the soul is partless and hence has no locality in it, and as the mind is ever in contact with it, the consequent illogicality of admitting any law regarding the origination of memory becomes insurmountable. Besides, one has to imagine that the Self can have the attribute of coming in contact with others, which idea is repugnant to the Vedas and the Smṛtis; for such are the two Vedic and Smṛti texts: 'Unattached, for It is never attached' (Bṛ. III. ix. 26), 'It is unconnected, and is the supporter of all' (G. XIII. 14). Moreover, since logic demands that a thing that has attributes, and is not of a different category, can come into contact with another having attributes, therefore it is illogical to hold that the Self which is attributeless, undifferentiated, and distinct from everything else, can come into contact with anything whatsoever that does not belong to the same category. Hence if the Self is the witness of all cognitions, then and not otherwise is established the idea that the Self, which is an effulgence that is in reality eternal and undecaying knowledge, is Brahman. Therefore the expression *pratibodha-viditam* has the meaning as explained by us.

As for the explanation, 'The expression, *pratibodha-viditam* means that the Self is known to oneself', it is possible where difference is imagined in a context in which the Self appears as a conditioned thing through identification with the limiting adjunct, intellect, so as to have such apparent activities as knowing the Self by the self (referred to in the texts): 'Sees the Self in his own self.' (Bṛ. IV. iv. 23), 'O Puruṣottama (lit. Supreme Puruṣa, i.e. Being), you yourself know your Self through the self' (G. X. 15). But in a context where the unconditioned Self is one, there can neither be knowing by oneself nor by another. Besides, It being by nature Consciousness Itself, there can be no dependence on another consciousness, just as a light does not depend on another light.

If the fact of being known to oneself is held in accordance with the Buddhist theory, then knowledge becomes momentary and is left without a Self (Reality); and this will contradict such Vedic texts as: 'For the knower's function of knowing can never be lost, because it is immortal'. (Bṛ. IV. iii. 30), 'Eternal, multiformed, all-pervading' (Mu. I. i. 6), 'That great birthless Self is undecaying, immortal, undying, fearless' (Bṛ. IV. iv. 25).

Others, again, imagine that by the word *pratibodha* is meant the uncaused knowledge as in the case of a sleeping man; according to still others, *pratibodha* is the knowledge that flashes but once.[1] (To this we say): Whether it be caused or uncaused, and whether it flashes once or twice, it is *pratibodha* to be sure.

Hi, because; *vindate*, (one) attains; *amṛtatvam*, immortality, existence in one's own Self, emancipation—by virtue of the aforesaid *pratibodha*, i.e. from the knowledge of the Self as appearing with reference to (i.e. as the witness of) each state of consciousness, therefore, the idea is that the Self is truly known when It is known along with each state of consciousness. Besides, consciousness, as having the indwelling Self as its content, is alone held to be the cause of immortality. Immortality does not surely consist in the Self becoming a non-Self. Immortality being the very nature of the Self, it is certainly without any cause. And thus mortality consists in the Self being perceived as the non-Self through ignorance.

How, again, is immortality attained through the aforesaid knowledge of the Self? This is being answered. *Ātmanā*, through one's own Self; *vindate*, (one) attains; *vīryam*, strength, capacity. The strength got from wealth, friend, incantation, medicine, asuterity, or Yoga cannot conquer death, for it is produced by impermanent things. But the strength, consequent on the knowledge of the Self, is acquired through the

[1] 'Once the unchanging Self is realized, there can no more be any knowership and therefore, no possibility of further knowledge. Hence the knowledge that flashes but once and becomes the cause of immediate emancipation is called *pratibodha*,'—Ā.G.

Self alone and not through anything else. Thus, since the strength resulting from the knowledge of the Self is independent of any means of acquisition, that strength alone is able to conquer death. Since the strength produced by the knowledge of the Self is thus attained through the Self, therefore, *vidyayā*, through knowledge about the Self; (one) *vindate*, attains; *amṛtam*, immortality. In the Upaniṣad of the AtharvaVeda it is said, 'This Self is not attained by one who has no strength (resulting from steadfastness in the Self)' (Mu. III. ii. 4). Therefore the statement of the reason, 'because thereby one attains immortality', is quite appropriate.

Pitiable, indeed, it is to suffer through ignorance, birth, old age, death, disease, etc., among multitudes of beings such as gods, men, animals, ghosts, etc., in whom there is an abundance of misery natural to transmigratory existence. Therefore,

इह चेदवेदीदथ सत्यमस्ति
न चेदिहावेदीन्महती विनष्टिः ।
भूतेषु भूतेषु विचित्य धीराः
प्रेत्यास्माल्लोकादमृता भवन्ति ॥५॥

इति केनोपनिषदि द्वितीयः खण्डः ॥

5. If one has realized here, then there is truth; if he has not realized here, then there is great destruction. The wise ones, having realized (Brahman) in

all beings, and having turned away from this world, become immortal.

Cet, if—a man having scriptural sanction and ability; *avedīt*, has known—the Self as defined and in the manner already explained; *iha*, here, indeed; *atha*, then; *asti satyam*, there is truth, there subsist in this human birth the values consisting in long life, wealth, and holiness,[1] or supreme reality. *Iha*, here, even while living, *cet*, if; a competent man *na avedīt*, has not realized; then there is *mahatī*, great interminable; *vinaṣṭiḥ*, destruction, transmigratory existence consisting in non-cessation of a continuous succession of birth, old age, death, etc. Therefore the *dhīrāḥ*, wise, Brāhmaṇas (the knowers of Brahman), who are thus familiar with merits and demerits; *vicitya*, having known, realized, the one reality on the Self; *bhūteṣu bhūteṣu*, in all beings, moving and unmoving; *pretya*, turning away, desisting; *asmāt lokāt*, from this world of ignorance—the world consisting of 'I and mine'—i.e. having attained the non-dual state consisting in becoming identified with the Self of all; *amṛtāḥ bhavanti*, become immortal, become Brahman indeed—this is the idea; as it has been said in the Vedic text: 'He who knows that supreme Brahman becomes Brahman indeed' (Mu. III. ii. 9).

[1] 'This is said by way of eulogy. (The idea is that) even worldly reality (or value), comprising long life (*avināśa*), wealth (*arthavattā*), holiness (*sadbhāva*), and fame, comes to the knower of Brahman (as a by-product). In reality, the result consisting in being established in Brahman follows as a necessary consequence.' —Ā.G.

PART III

ब्रह्म ह देवेभ्यो विजिग्ये तस्य ह ब्रह्मणो विजये देवा अमहीयन्त ॥१॥

1. It was Brahman, indeed, that achieved victory for the sake of the gods. In that victory which was in fact Brahman's, the gods became elated.

After hearing the text, 'unknown to those who know well, and known to those who do not know' etc. (II. 3), some people of dull intellect may have this kind of delusion: 'It is seen that whatever exists is known through the valid means of cognition; and whatever does not exist remains unknown, is like the horns of a hare, and absolutely non-existent. Similarly this Brahman, being unknown, is certainly non-existent.' Lest there be this delusion, this story is begun. For the subsequent passages are seen to be leading to this conclusion: 'Since that very Brahman is the ruler in every way, the supreme Deity of even the deities, the supreme Lord over the lordly beings, inscrutable, the cause of the victory of gods, and the cause of the defeat of the devils, therefore, how can It be non-existent?' Or the story is meant to eulogize the knowledge of Brahman. How? By saying that it was surely by virtue of the knowledge of Brahman, that Fire and other gods attained supremacy over the gods, and Indra got still greater pre-eminence. Or (through the story) it is shown that Brahman is inscrutable, inasmuch as Fire and others, powerful though they are, knew Brahman with sheer difficulty, and so also did Indra, even though he is the ruler of the gods. Or the whole thing is meant to enjoin an injunction regarding the secret teachings (about meditations) that will follow[1] (IV. 4-7). Or the story is meant to show, that apart from the knowledge of Brahman, all notions of agentship etc. that creatures possess, as for instance the conceit of the gods with regard to victory etc., are false.

Brahma, the supreme Brahman already spoken of; *ha*, verily; *devebhyaḥ*, for the sake of the gods; *vijigye*, achieved victory. In a fight between the gods and the devils, Brahman, after conquering the devils, the enemies of the world and transgressors of divine rules, gave to the gods the victory and its results for ensuring the stability of the world. *Tasya ha Brahmaṇaḥ vijaye*, in that victory which was, indeed, Brahman's; *devāḥ*, the gods, Fire etc.; *amahīyanta*, became elated.

त ऐक्षन्तास्माकमेवायं विजयोऽस्माकमेवायं महिमेति। तद्धैषां विजज्ञौ तेभ्यो ह प्रादुर्बभूव तन्न व्यजानत किमिदं यक्षमिति ॥२॥

2. They thought, 'Ours, indeed, is this victory, ours, indeed, is this glory,' Brahman knew this pre-

[1] 'The realization of the Self as Brahman, which is meant for the most advanced ones and which is not an object of knowledge, has been spoken of earlier. Later will be stated the meditation on the qualified Brahman which is for the less advanced people. The following passages present that meditation, since the injunction for it is clearly to be seen (in IV.6-7). So the real significance lies in this. As for the other interpretations (advanced by Saṅkara), they are merely by way of showing posibilities.' —Ā.G.

tension of theirs. To them It did appear. They could not make out about that thing,[1] as to what this Yakṣa (venerable Being) might be.

Then, not knowing that this victory and this glory belonged to God who sits in the hearts as the indwelling Self—omniscient, dispenser of the fruits of all works of all creatures, omnipotent, and desirous of encompassing the stability of the world—*te*, they, those gods; *aikṣanta*, thought; '*Ayam vijayaḥ*, this victory; is *eva asmākam*, indeed ours, is of ourselves, who are limited by our personalities as Fire and others. *Asmākam eva*, ours indeed, and not of God as our indwelling Self; is *ayam mahimā*, this glory evidenced by such states as of Fire, Air, Indra, etc. which is experienced by us as the result of victory. This has not been achieved by God who is our indwelling Self.' Brahman *ha*, surely; *vijajñau*, knew; *tat*, that, that erroneous deliberation of those whose thoughts were being directed by a false self-conceit; for Brahman is omniscient by virtue of being the director of the senses of all creatures. Noticing this false idea of the gods, and thinking, 'In order that the gods may not be thus defeated like the devils, as a consequence of their vainglory, I shall, out of grace for them, favour the gods by removing their presumptuousness'—with this idea, It, *ha*, indeed; for their sake, *prādurbabhūva*, appeared as an object of perception; *tebhyaḥ*, to the gods; through an unprecedentedly wonderful and astonishing form created by Brahman's own power

[1] Could not solve this riddle about Brahman appearing in the form of Yakṣa.

of *Māyā*,[1] It appeared as an object of perception to the senses of the gods. The gods *na vyajānata*, did not comprehend; *tat*, that, the Brahman which had become manifest; *kim iti*, as to what; *idam yakṣam*, this venerable, great Being, might be.

तेऽग्निमब्रुवञ्जातवेद एतद्विजानीहि किमिदं यक्षमिति तथेति ॥३॥

3. They said to Fire, 'O Jātavedā, find out thoroughly about this thing as to what this Yakṣa is.' He said, 'So be it.'

Te, they—those gods who failed to know It, and were desirous of knowing It, but had fear in their hearts; *abruvan*, said; *agnim*, to Fire, (lit.) who goes ahead (of all); and who is *jātavedā*, almost omniscient:[2] O Jātavedā, you being powerful among us; *vijānīhi*, thoroughly find out about; *etat*, this Yakṣa that is in our view; *kim etat yakṣam iti*, as to what this Yakṣa (venerable Being) is.

तदभ्यद्रवत्तमभ्यवदत्कोऽसीत्यग्निर्वा अहमस्मीत्यब्रवीज्जातवेदा वा अहमस्मीति ॥४॥

4. To It he went. To him It said, 'Who are you?' He said, 'I am known as Fire, or I am Jātavedā,'

[1] 'The *yoga*, or the combination of attributes—*Sattva*, *Rajas*, and *Tamas* is Māyā. Through the power of that.'—Ā.G.

[2] Agni precedes all other deities (*agre gacchati*) in receiving oblations at sacrifices; and Jātavedā is one who knows (*veda*) all that is created (*jāta*).

Saying, '*Tathā*, so be it', *iti*, this much; Fire *abhi-adravat*, approached, moved, towards It, *tat*, towards that Yakṣa. *Tam*, to him, to Fire, who had approached and was desirous of asking, but had become silent because of absence of arrogance in Its presence; the Yakṣa, *abhyavadat*, said; '*Kaḥ asi iti*, who are you?' Thus being asked by Brahman, Fire said, '*Agniḥ vai*, I am Fire (*agni*) by name, and am also familiarly known as Jātavedā', showing thereby his self-importance consisting in his being well known through the two names.

तस्मिꣳस्त्वयि किं वीर्यमित्यपीदꣳ सर्वं दहेयं यदिदं पृथिव्यामिति ॥५॥

5. (It said), 'What power is there in you, such as you are?' (Fire said), 'I can burn up all this that is on the earth.'

To him who had spoken thus, Brahman said, '*Tasmin tvayi*, in you who are such, who possess such famous names and attributes; *kim vīryam*, what power, what ability, is there?' He replied, '*Daheyam*, I can burn up, reduce to ashes; *idam sarvam*, all this creation that moves and does not move; *pṛthivyām*, on this earth.' The word *pṛthivyām* is used illustratively (to indicate everything), for even things that are in the region above the earth are surely consumed by fiire.

तस्मै तृणं निदधावेतद्दहेति । तदुपप्रेयाय सर्वजवेन तन्न शशाक दग्धुं स तत एव निववृते नैतदशकं विज्ञातुं यदेतद्यक्षमिति ॥६॥

6. (Yakṣa) placed a straw for him saying, 'Burn this.' (Fire) approached the straw with the power born of full enthusiasm. He could not consume it. He returned from the Yakṣa (to tell the gods), 'I could not ascertain It fully as to what this Yakṣa is.'

Tasmai, for him who had such presumption; Brahman *tṛṇam nidadhau*, placed a straw, in front of Fire. Being told by Brahman, '*Etat*, this mere straw; *daha*, burn, in my front. If you are not able to burn it, give up your vanity as a consumer everywhere.' (Fire) *tat upapreyāya*, went near that straw; *sarvajavena*, with the speed born of the fullest enthusiasm. Going there, *tat*, that thing; *na śaśāka dagdhum*, he could not burn. That Fire, being unable to burn the straw and becoming ashamed and foiled in his promise, silently *nivavṛte*, withdrew; *tataḥ eva*, from that Yakṣa; and went back towards the gods (to tell them), '*Na aśakam*, I did not succeed; *vijñātum*, in knowing fully; *etat*, this Yakṣa: *yat etat yakṣam*, as to what this Yakṣa is.'

अथ वायुमब्रुवन्वायवेतद्विजानीहि किमेतद्यक्षमिति तथेति ॥७॥

7. Then (the gods) said to Air, 'O Air, find out thoroughly about this thing as to what this Yakṣa is.' (Air said), 'So be it.'

तदभ्यद्रवत्तमभ्यवदत्कोऽसीति वायुर्वा अहमस्मीत्यब्रवीन्मातरिश्वा वा अहमस्मीति ॥८॥

8. To It he went. To him It said, 'Who are you?' He said, 'I am known as Air, or I am Mātariśvā.'

तस्मिꣳस्त्वयि किं वीर्यमित्यपीदꣳ सर्वमाददीय यदिदं पृथिव्यामिति ॥९॥

9. (It said), 'What power is there in you, such as you are?' (Air said), 'I can blow away all this that is on the earth.'

तस्मै तृणं निदधावेतदादत्स्वेति तदुपप्रेयाय सर्वजवेन तन्न शशाकादातुं स तत एव निववृते नैतदशकं विज्ञातुं यदेतद्यक्षमिति ॥१०॥

10. (Yakṣa) placed a straw for him saying, 'Take it up.' Air approached the straw with all the strength born of enthusiasm. He could not take it up. He returned from that Yakṣa (to tell the gods), 'I could not ascertain It fully as to what this Yakṣa is.'

Atha, after that; they said to Air; 'O Air, find out' etc. bears the same meaning as before. Vāyu (air) is so called because it blows, goes, or carries smell. Mātariśvā means that which travels (*śvayati*) in space (*mātari*). *Idam sarvam api*, all this; *ādadīya*, I can take up, blow away. *Yad idam pṛthivyām* etc. is just as explained earlier.

अथेन्द्रमब्रुवन्मघवन्नेतद्विजानीहि किमेतद्यक्षमिति तथेति तदभ्यद्रवत्तस्मात्तिरोदधे ॥११॥

11. Then (the gods) said to Indra, 'O Maghavā, find out thoroughly about this thing, as to what this

Yakṣa is.' (He said), 'So be it.' He (Indra) approached It (Yakṣa). From him (Yakṣa) vanished away.

Atha indram abruvan maghavan etat vijānīhi etc. is to be explained as before. Indr , who is a great Lord and is called Maghavā because of strength, *tat abhyadravat*, approached that Yakṣa. *Tasmāt*, from him, from Indra who had approached Itself (Yakṣa); that Brahman, *tirodadhe*, vanished from sight. Brahman did not so much as grant him an interview, so that Indra's pride at being Indra might be totally eradicated.

स तस्मिन्नेवाकाशे स्त्रियमाजगाम बहुशोभमानामुमाꣳ हैमवतीं ताꣳहोवाच किमेतद्यक्षमिति ॥१२॥

12. In that very space he approached her, the superbly charming woman, viz Umā Haimavatī[1]. To Her (he said), 'What is this Yakṣa?'

The space, or the part of the space where that Yakṣa vanished after revealing Itself, and the space where Indra also was at the time of the disappearance of Brahman, *tasmin eva ākāśe*, in that very space; *saḥ*, he, Indra, stayed on, deliberating in his mind, 'What is this Yakṣa?' He did not return like Fire etc. Understanding his devotion to Yakṣa, Knowledge (of Brahman) made Her appearance as a woman, in the form of Umā. *Saḥ*, he, Indra; *ājagāma*, approached;

[1] The superbly fascinating (*haimavatī*) knowledge of Brahman (Umā), or the daughter of Himalayas, whose name was Umā.

tām, Her, Umā; who was *bahuśobhamānām*, superbly charming—Knowledge being the most fascinating of all fascinating things, the attribute 'superbly charming' is appropriate for it. He approached her, *haimavatīm*, who was as though attired in dress of gold, i.e. exquisitely beautiful. Or, Umā Herself is Haimavatī, the daughter of Himavat (Himalayas). Thinking that, since She is ever in association with the omniscient God, She must be able to know, Indra approached Her; (and) *tām*, to Her, to Umā; *uvāca*, said, 'Tell me, *kim etat yakṣam iti*, what is this Yakṣa—that showed Itself and vanished?'

PART IV

सा ब्रह्मेति होवाच ब्रह्मणो वा एतद्विजये महीयध्वमिति ततो हैव विदाञ्चकार ब्रह्मेति ॥१॥

1. 'It was Brahman', said She. 'In Brahman's victory, indeed, you became elated thus.' From that (utterance) alone, to be sure, did Indra learn that It was Brahman.

Sā, She; *uvāca ha*, said, '*Brahma iti*, It was Brahman. *Brahmaṇaḥ vai vijaye*, in the victory of God, indeed: The devils were conquered only by God, and you were mere instruments there. In the victory that was really His, you *mahīyadhvam*, became elated, you attained glory.' The word *etat*, in this way, is used adverbially (to modify the verb). 'But yours is this vaingloriousness: "(*Asmākam eva ayam vijayaḥ, asmākam eva ayam mahimā*)—ours is this victory, ours is this glory"' (III. 2). *Tataḥ ha eva*, from that, from that utterance of Umā, to be sure; Indra, *vidāṁcakāra*, learned; *brahma iti*, that It was Brahman. The emphatic limitation implied in *tataḥ ha eva*, from that alone, to be sure, implies (that he came to learn) not independently.

तस्माद्वा एते देवा अतितरामिवान्यान्देवान्यदग्निर्वायुरिन्द्रस्ते ह्येनन्नेदिष्ठं पस्पर्शुस्ते ह्येनत्प्रथमो विदाञ्चकार ब्रह्मेति ॥२॥

2. Therefore, indeed, these gods, viz Fire, Air,

and Indra, did excel other gods, for they indeed touched It most proximately, and they knew It first as Brahman.

Since these gods—Fire, Air, and Indra—approached Brahman through conversation, visualization, etc., *tasmāt*, therefore; *ete devāḥ*, these gods; *atitarām iva*, surpassed greatly, through their own excellence, i.e. good luck comprising power, quality, etc.; *anyān devān*, the other gods. The word *iva* is meaningless or is used for the sake of emphasis. *Yat agniḥ vāyuḥ indraḥ*, for, (the gods) viz Fire, Air and Indra; *te*, they, those gods; *hi*, indeed, *nediṣṭham paspar-śuḥ*,[1] most proximately, intimately, touched; *enat*, this Brahman, through the process of conversation etc. with Brahman, as described earlier. *Hi*, because, because of the further reason that; *te* they; being *prathamaḥ* (should be *prathamāḥ*) first, i.e. being prominent; *vidāṁcakāra*, (should be *vidāṁcakruḥ*), knew; *enat*, It, Brahman,—that 'this is Brahman.'

तस्माद्वा इन्द्रोऽतितरामिवान्यान्देवान्स ह्येनन्नेदिष्ठं पस्पर्श स ह्येनत्प्रथमो विदाञ्चकार ब्रह्मेति ॥३॥

3. Therefore did Indra excel the other deities. For he touched It most proximately, inasmuch as he knew It first as Brahman.

Since even Fire and Air knew from the words of Indra alone, and since Indra heard first from Umā's

[1] A different reading is *paspṛśuḥ*.

words that It was Brahman, *tasmāt vai indraḥ atitarām iva*, therefore, Indra did excel (the other deities). *Hi saḥ enat nediṣṭham pasparśa*, for he touched It most proximately; *saḥ hi enat prathamaḥ vidāṁcakāra brahma iti*—this sentence has been already explained.

तस्यैष आदेशो यदेतद्विद्युतो व्यद्युतदा३ इतीन् न्यमीमिषदा३ इत्यधिदैवतम् ॥४॥

4. This is Its instruction (about meditation) through analogy. It is like that which is (known as) the flash of lightning, and It is also as though the eye winked. These are (illustrations) in a divine context.[1]

Tasya, of the Brahman under discussion; *eṣaḥ ādeśaḥ*, this is the instruction through analogy. That analogy through which the instruction about the incomparable Brahman is imparted is called *ādeśaḥ*. What is that? *Yat etat*, that fact, which is well known among people as the flash of lightning. Since *vidyutaḥ vyadyutat*, cannot mean that Brahman flashed (*vyadyutat*) (by borrowing Its light) from lightning, (*vidyutaḥ*)[2] therefore the meaning has to be assumed to be 'the flash of lightning.' *Ā*, like, is used in the sense of com-

[1] Analogies with regard to Brahman as It exists in Its divine, but conditioned, form in the solar orb. Cf. *Gītā*, VIII.4. Brahman in Its form as Hiraṇyagarbha resides in the solar orb and presides over all the deities that are but Its different manifestations.

[2] 'The meaning, "It flashed from lightning", is inadmissible, for Brahman being self-effulgent, Its effulgence cannot be dependent on others. The meaning, "It performed the flashing of lightning," is unacceptable, since the flash that belongs to something cannot be produced by another.'—Ā.G.

parison. The meaning is: 'It is like the flash of lightning'; and (this meaning is acceptable) since it is seen in a different Vedic text, 'comparable to a single flash of lightning' (Bṛ. II. iii. 6); for Brahman disappeared after revealing Itself but once to the gods like lightning. Or the word *tejaḥ* (brilliance) has to be supplied after the word *vidyutaḥ* (of lightning). *Vyadyutat* (in this case) means, flashed; (and) *ā* means as it were. The purport is: It was as though, the brilliance of lightning flashed but once. The word *iti* is meant to call back to memory the word *ādeśa*; (so the meaning is): This is the *ādeśa*, the analogy. The word *it* is used for joining together. (So the sense is): Here is another analogy for It. What is that one? *Nyamīmiṣat*, winked, as the eye did the act of winking. The causative form (in *nyamīmiṣat*) is used in the same sense as the root itself. The *ā* is used here, too, in the sense of comparison. The meaning is: And it was like the opening and shutting of the eye with regard to its object. *Iti adhidaivatam*, this is by way of showing analogies of Brahman in a divine context.

अथाध्यात्मं यदेतद्गच्छतीव च मनोऽनेन चैतदुपस्मरत्यभीक्ष्ण ँ सङ्कल्पः ॥५॥

5. Then is the instruction through analogy in the context of the (individual) self: This known fact, that the mind seems to go to It (Brahman), and the fact that It (Brahman) is repeatedly remembered through the mind; as also the thought, (that the mind has with regard to Brahman).

Atha, after this; is being told the analogical instruction *adhyātmam*, in the context of the soul, with regard to the indwelling Self. *Yat etat*, that which is a known fact; viz that *etat*, to this Brahman; *gacchati iva ca manaḥ*, though the mind goes, as it were, the mind enters into Brahman, as it were, encompasses It as an object. And the fact that *anena*, by that mind; the spiritual aspirant; *abhīkṣṇam*, repeatedly; *upasmarati*, remembers intimately; *etat*, this Brahman; and the *saṅkalpaḥ*, thought of the mind with regard to Brahman. Since Brahman has got the mind as Its limiting adjunct, It seems to be revealed by such states of the mind as thought, memory, etc., by which It seems to be objectified. Therefore this is an instruction about Brahman, through analogy, in the context of the soul. In the divine context, Brahman has the attribute of revealing Itself quickly like lightning and winking[1]; and in the context of the soul, It has the attribute of manifesting Itself simultaneously with the states of the mind.[2] This is the instruction about

[1] 'The winking of the eye is rapid—this is well known; similar is Brahman's power of acting quickly. Its attribute in the divine context is the power to act quickly with regard to creation etc., since there is an absence of obstruction and effort. . . . The light of lightning covers the whole world at once. Similarly Brahman is unsurpassingly bright by nature, and It accomplishes creation etc. of everything quickly, and It is possessed of supreme glory.'—Ā.G.

[2] 'One should meditate thus: "Towards this Brahman, that is of the nature of light, my mind proceeds and there it rests." The instruction in this form is the instruction in the context of the individual soul. The indwelling Brahman becomes revealed to one who meditates thus: "The thoughts in my mind constantly revolve round Brahman."'—Ā.G.

Brahman through analogy. The need for this teaching about Brahman through analogy is that It becomes easily comprehensible to people of dull intellect when instruction is thus imparted. For the unconditioned Brahman, as such, cannot be comprehended by people of dull intellect.

तद्ध तद्वनं नाम तद्वनमित्युपासितव्यं स य एतदेवं वेदाभि हैनँ सर्वाणि भूतानि संवाञ्छन्ति ॥६॥

6. The Brahman is well known as the one adorable to all creatures: (hence) It is to be meditated on with the help of the name *tadvana.* All creatures surely pray to anyone who meditates on It in this way.

Further, *tat*, that Brahman; is *ha*, certainly; *tadvanam nāma*: *tadvanam* is derived from the words *tasya*, his, and *vanam*, adorable; It is adorable to all creatures, since It is their indwelling Self. Therefore Brahman is *tadvanam nāma*, well known as the one to be adored by all beings. Since it is *tadvana*, therefore *tadvanam iti*, through this very name, *tadvana*, which is indicative of Its quality; It is *upāsitavyam*, to be meditated on. The text states the results of meditation[1] through this name; *saḥ yaḥ*, anyone who; *veda*, meditates on; *etat*, the aforesaid Brahman; *evam*, thus, as possessed of the qualities mentioned above; *sarvāṇi bhūtāni*, all beings; *ha*, certainly; *enam*, to him, this meditator; *abhisamvāñchanti*, pray, as (they do) to Brahman.

[1] In place of '*upāswasya*, of meditation', some read '*upāsakasya*, to the meditator'.

उपनिषदं भो ब्रूहीत्युक्ता त उपनिषद्ब्राह्मीं वाव त उपनिषदमब्रूमेति ॥७॥

7. (Disciple: 'Sir, speak of the secret knowledge.' (Teacher): 'I have told you of the secret knowledge; I have imparted to you that very secret knowledge of Brahman.'

After being instructed thus, the disciple said to the teacher, '*Bhoḥ*, sir; *brūhi*, speak of *upaniṣadam*, the secret thing that is to be thought about'; *iti*. To the student who had spoken thus, the teacher said, '*Te*, to you; *upaniṣad*, the secret knowledge; *uktā*, has been spoken of.' 'What is that again?'—to such a question he answers, '*Te*, to you; *upaniṣadam vāva abrūma iti*, I have spoken this very secret; *brāhmīm*, relating to Brahman, to the supreme Self—since the knowledge already imparted relates to the supreme Self.' For the sake of (distinguishing) what follows, the teacher delimits (his teaching) thus: 'The Upaniṣad that I have told you consists of nothing but what has already been presented as the Upaniṣad of the supreme Self.'

Objection: What motive could have prompted the disciple, who had heard the Upaniṣad about the supreme Self, to put this question: 'Sir, speak of the Upaniṣad'? If, now, the question related to what had been already heard, then it is useless, inasmuch as it involved a repetition like the grinding over again of what had already been ground. If, again, the earlier Upaniṣad was incomplete, then it was not proper to conclude it by mentioning its result thus: 'Having turned away from this world, the intelligent ones become immortal' (II. 5). Hence the question is surely improper even if it relates to some unexplained portion of the Upaniṣad already presented, inasmuch as no remainder was left over. What then is the intention of the questioner?

Answer: We say that this is the intention (of the disciple): 'Does the secret teaching already imparted need anything as an accessory, or does it not need any? If it does, tell me of the secret teaching with regard to that needed accessory. Or if it does not, then like Pippalāda make the clinching assertion: "There is nothing beyond this" (Pr. VI. 7).' Thus this clincher of the teacher; 'I have told you the Upaniṣad' is justified.

Objection: May it not be urged that this is not a concluding remark, inasmuch as the teacher has something more to add in the statement: 'Concentration, cessation from sense-objects, rites, etc. are its legs' etc. (IV. 8).

Answer: It is true that a fresh matter is introduced by the teacher; but this is not done either by way of bringing in something as an attributive constituent (*śeṣa*) of the Upaniṣad or as an accessory (*sahakārī*) to it,[1] but rather as a means for the acquisition of the knowledge of Brahman, because *tapas* (concentration) etc., occurring as they do in the same passage along with the Vedas and their supplementaries, are given

[1] 'By the word *śeṣa* is implied an attributive part contributing to the production of the effect (of the main rite). By the word *sahakārī* is implied something that need not necessarily be a constituent, but can be combined (with the principal rite).'—Ā.G. Both have a bearing on the result.

an equal status with the latter, and because neither the Vedas nor the science of pronunciation and euphony (*śikṣā*) etc., which are their supplementaries, can directly be either attributive constituents of the knowledge of Brahman or its helpful accessories.

Objection: Should not even things that occur in the same passage be put to separate uses according to their appropriateness? Just as the *mantras*, occurring at the end of a sacrifice, in the form of a hymn meant for the invocation of (many) deities, are applied with respect to the individual deities concerned, similarly it can be imagined that concentration, self-control, rites, truth, etc., will either be attributive constituents of the knowledge of Brahman or be helpful accessories (in accordance with their respective appropriateness).[1] As for the Vedas and their subsidiaries, they are means for either knowledge of the Self or rites by virtue of their respective meanings (ideas). In this way this division becomes appropriate when significance of words, relation (of things denoted), and reason are taken into consideration. Suppose we advance such an argument?

[1] At the end of all sacrifices, the deities are invoked with the hymn beginning with:

अग्निरिदं हविरजुषतावीवृधत महो ज्यायोऽकृत ।
अग्नीषोमाविदं हविरजुषेतामवीवृधेतां महो ज्यायोऽक्राताम् ॥

Now although in this hymn many deities are mentioned, still, it is proper to invoke at the end the deity to whom any particular sacrifice is made, the hymn itself has to be applied in accord with that propriety. Similarly concentration etc., will themselves be used as attributive constituents of knowledge.' —Ā.G.

Answer: No, because this is illogical. This division does not certainly accord with facts, because it is not reasonable that the knowledge of Brahman, which repels all ideas of distinction of deeds, doers, and results, should have dependence on any attributive constituent, or any relation with any helpful accessory, and because the knowledge of Brahman and its result, freedom, are concerned only with the Self which is unassociated with any object. 'He who wants emancipation should for ever give up all works together with their instruments, because it is known only by the man of renunciation. The state of the supreme Reality that is the same as the indwelling Self is attained by the man of renunciation.' Therefore knowledge cannot reasonably have work either as an accessory or as a complement. Therefore the division of (concentration etc.) on the analogy of the invocation through hymn, occurring at the end of a sacrifice, is quite inappropriate. Hence it is proper to say that the question and the answer are meant for fixing a limit thus: 'The secret teaching that has been imparted extends thus far only; it is adequate for the attainment of knowledge without depending on anything else.'

तस्यै तपो दमः कर्मेति प्रतिष्ठा वेदाः सर्वाङ्गानि सत्य-
मायतनम् ॥८॥

8. Concentration, cessation from sense-objects, rites, etc., are its legs; the Vedas are all its limbs; truth is its abode.

Concentration etc. are the means for the acquisition, *tasyai*, (should be *tasyāḥ*), of that secrét teaching (Upaniṣad), regarding Brahman which I thus spoke before you. *Tapaḥ*, the concentration of the body, the senses, and the mind; *damaḥ*, cessation (from sense-objects); *karma*, rites, Agnihotra etc. (are the means); for it is found that the knowledge of Brahman arises in a man who has attained the requisite holiness by means of purification of the heart through these. For it is a matter of experience that, even though Brahman is spoken of, there is either non-comprehension or miscomprehension in the case of one who has not been purged of his sin, as for instance, in the cases of Indra and Virocana (Ch. VIII. vii-xii). Therefore knowledge, as imparted by the Vedas, dawns on one whose mind has been purified by concentration etc., either in this life or in many past ones, as is mentioned by the Vedic verse: 'These things get revealed when spoken to that high-souled man who has supreme devotion towards the Effulgent One, and the same devotion to his teacher as to the Effulgent One' (Śv. VI. 23). And this is borne out by the Smṛti, 'Knowledge dawns on a man on the eradication of sinful acts.' (Mbh.Śā. 204.8). The word *iti* is used to draw attention to a synecdoche; that is to say, by the word *iti* are suggested other factors, beginning with these, which are helpful to the rise of knowledge, such as 'Humility, unpretentiousness,' etc. (G. xiii. 7). (Concentration etc. are the) *pratiṣṭhā*, two legs, stands as it were, of this (Upaniṣad); for when these exist, knowledge of Brahman stands firm and becomes active, just as a man does with his legs. *Vedāḥ*, the four Vedas; and *sarvāṅgāni*, all the six subsidiaries beginning with the science of pronunciation and euphony (*śikṣā*) (are also the legs). The Vedas are the legs because they reveal the rites and knowledge; and all the *aṅgāni*, subsidiaries, are so because they are meant for the protection of the Vedas. Or since the word *pratiṣṭhā* has been imagined to imply the two legs (of the knowledge), the Vedas are its *sarvāṅgāni*, all the other limbs beginning with the head. In this case, the subsidiaries, such as the science of pronunciation and euphony, are to be understood to have been mentioned by the word Vedas; because when the principal factor is mentioned, the subsidiaries are mentioned *ipso facto*, they being dependent on the principal. *Satyam āyatanam*, *satya* is the *āyatana*, the dwelling place where the secret teaching resides. *Satya* means freedom from deceit and crookedness in speech, mind, and body; for knowledge abides in those who are free from deceit and who are holy, and not in those who are devilish by nature and are deceitful, as the Vedic text says, 'those in whom there are no crookedness falsehood and deceit' (Pr. I. 16). Therefore *satya* (truth) is imagined as the abode. Although by implication, truth has already been mentioned as legs, along with concentration etc., still its allusion again as the abode is for indicating that, as a means (for the acquisition of knowledge) it excels others, as the Smṛti says, 'A thousand horse-sacrifices and truth are weighed in a balance: and one truth outweighs a thousand horse-sacrifices' (V. Sm. 8).

यो वा एतामेवं वेदापहत्य पाप्मानमनन्ते स्वर्गे लोके ज्येये प्रतितिष्ठति प्रतितिष्ठति ॥९॥

इति केनोपनिषदि चतुर्थः खण्डः ॥

9. Anyone who knows this thus, he, having dispelled sin, remains firmly seated in the boundless, blissful, and highest Brahman. He remains firmly seated (there).

Yaḥ vai, anyone who; *veda evam*, realizes thus—as spoken; *etām*, this thing, this blessed knowledge of Brahman which has been already spoken of in the text beginning with 'Willed by whom' (I. 1), which has been eulogized in the text beginning with, 'It was Brahman indeed' (III. 1), and which is 'the basis of all knowledge' (Mu. I. i. 1)—. Notwithstanding the presentation of the fruit of the knowledge of Brahman in 'because thereby one gets immortality' (II. 4), it is mentioned at the end by way of a formal conclusion:—(Such a knower) *apahatya pāpmānam*, dispelling sin, shaking off the seed of mundane existence constituted by ignorance, desire, and work; *pratitiṣṭhati*, remains firmly seated; *anante*, in the boundless; *svarge loke*: *Svarge loke* means in Brahman who is all Bliss. Being qualified by the word *ananta*, boundless, the word *svarga* does not mean heaven. Lest the word boundless (*ananta*), be taken in any secondary sense, the text says *jyeye*, in the higher, that which is greater than all, in one's own Self which is boundless in the primary sense. The purport is that he does not again return to this world.

ॐ आप्यायन्तु ममाङ्गानि वाक्प्राणश्चक्षुः श्रोत्रमथो बलमिन्द्रियाणि च सर्वाणि। सर्वं ब्रह्मौपनिषदं माऽहं ब्रह्म निराकुर्यां मा मा ब्रह्म निराकरोदनिराकरणमस्त्वनिराकरणं मेऽस्तु। तदात्मनि निरते य उपनिषत्सु धर्मास्ते मयि सन्तु ते मयि सन्तु।

ॐ शान्तिः शान्तिः शान्तिः ॥

INDEX TO ŚLOKAS

Bhagavad-Gita

With the Commentary of Madhusudana Sarasvati
Translated by Swami Gambhirananda

pp. 1038 Rs. 185

The present work of Madhusudana Sarasvati, the *Gudhartha Dipika* (an Annotation revealing the true import of the *Gita*) is probably the greatest of his many literary works. Though there are many classical commentaries on the *Gita*, this work stands next only to Sri Shankaracharya's commentary as regards clarity, depth, and originality.

This book is a valuable addition to our publications and is highly recommended to serious students of Indian philosophy and religion.

81750 50683

Rs. 14

68-3

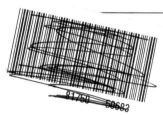